Tell Me About Turtles

Kristine Lalley

Rosen Classroom Books & Materials
New York

1

A turtle comes from an egg.

shell

A turtle has a shell.

A turtle can be little.

A turtle can be big.

Some turtles live on land.

Some turtles live in water.

Words to Know

shell

turtle